This book is to be retur...
the last date stamped b.

PROJEC

We Love PASSOVER

Saviour Pirotta

WAYLAND

Editor: Kirsty Hamilton
Senior Design Manager: Rosamund Saunders
Designer: Elaine Wilkinson

Published in Great Britain in 2006 by Wayland,
an imprint of Hachette Children's Books

The right of Saviour Pirotta to be identified as the author of
the work has been asserted by him in the Copyright, Designs
and Patents Act 1988.

British Library Cataloguing in Publication Data
Pirotta, Saviour
We love Passover
1.Passover - Juvenile literature
I.Title
394.2'67

ISBN: 0 7502 4838 6
ISBN 13: 978-0-7502-4838-9

Printed in China

Wayland
An imprint of Hachette Children's Books
338 Euston Road, London NW1 3BH

The publishers would like to thank the following for
allowing us to reproduce their pictures in this book:

Wayland Picture Library: 6, 12, 20 / Sonia Halliday: 5, 6, 7,
11 / Corbis: title page 21, Roger Ressmeyer; 23, Philip de
Bay / Alamy: 16, Steve Allan, 10, Eitan Simanor, 22, World
Religions Photo Library; 15, Network Photographers, 18,
Photofusion Picture Library / Getty Images: 4, Baerbel
Schmidt; 17, Formula Z/S; 9, Ancient Art and Architecture /
Art Directors: 13, Juliette Soester, 14, Itzhak Genut, 19,
Helene Rogers.

Contents

Shalom and welcome!

Welcome to Passover, the Jewish festival of freedom. At Passover, Jewish people remember when their **ancestors** escaped from Egypt. The festival starts on the 15th day of the Jewish month of Nissan.

The Jewish day begins at sunset the night before.

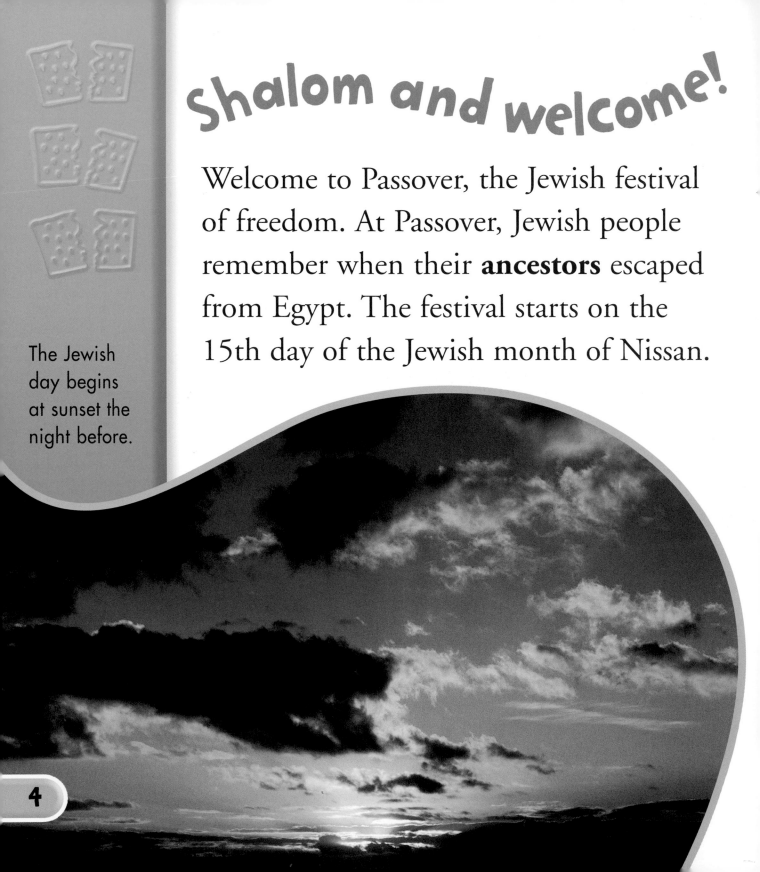

Look, the sun is setting.
A new day is beginning.
It is time
to start …

Jewish children play an important part in Passover.

5

Let my people go!

This painting shows Jewish slaves being forced to make bricks to build the **pyramids**.

A long time ago, the Jewish people had no freedom. They were slaves in Egypt. But God wanted them to be free.

A plague of
locusts ate
all the corn
in Egypt.

He ordered a Jewish shepherd called
Moses to demand their freedom but the
Egyptian **Pharaoh** would not let them
go. God sent ten **plagues** to punish
the Egyptians.

Passed over

It took one last punishment, a tenth plague, to convince the Pharaoh to free the Jewish slaves. The eldest boy in each Egyptian house was to die.

A mysterious disease killed all the Pharaoh's farm animals.

But God told the Jewish people to mark the doors of their houses with lamb's blood. That way Death 'passed over' their houses and the Jewish children were saved.

This illustration shows a man marking his door with lamb's blood.

Freedom at last

This baker is making dough to roll in to **matzah** for Passover.

When the Egyptians lost their eldest sons, the Pharaoh set the Jewish people free. The slaves left in such a hurry, there was no time to make bread for the journey. In the desert they baked flat loaves called **matzot**.

10

DID YOU KNOW?

Some Egyptians paid the Jewish people with gold and silver to leave Egypt.

Since then the flat loaves have become the symbol of Passover.

Matzot, like the ones these children are eating, are flat because they have no **yeast** in them.

11

cleaning out the house

No food with yeast in it is eaten during Passover. Before the festival starts, Jewish people get rid of all scraps of bread, cakes and biscuits.

Matzah and special Passover food can be found in shops before the festival.

DID YOU KNOW?

Special pots and utensils
are brought out to cook
Passover food.

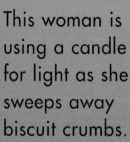

They even clean
their offices and shops.
Eating only food without
yeast reminds them of
the Jews fleeing Egypt.

This woman is
using a candle
for light as she
sweeps away
biscuit crumbs.

No more yeast

These people are dipping their kitchen utensils in boiling water to clean them for Passover.

The day before Passover, Jewish families do a final search in the house for food with yeast in it. If they find any, they put it in a bag and burn it.

Now the house is clean or '**kosher**'. The festival can begin.

These people have come together to burn their food with yeast in it.

15

Seder food

On each of the first two nights of Passover, Jewish people eat a meal called a **Seder**.

The foods of Seder are eaten in a special order.

פסח

16

On the table is a Seder plate with different foods on it. Each item of food reminds people of something about the Jews' escape from slavery in Egypt.

Parsley dipped in salty water reminds Jewish people how much their ancestors cried.

DID YOU KNOW?

A paste of apple and walnuts is a reminder of the cement the Jewish slaves used for building.

Retelling the story

During the Seder meal, the grown-ups read out loud from the **Haggadah**, the book that tells how the Jews escaped from Egypt. The book also has songs, prayers and blessings.

These people are dipping their fingers in red wine and spilling a drop on their plates in memory of the plagues.

This illustration is from the Haggadah. It shows the ten plagues that God sent to punish the Egyptians.

A drop of wine is spilt for each of the ten plagues. This shows how sad people are that their freedom caused the Egyptians a lot of pain and suffering.

19

Find the Matzah

Children look forward to finding the hidden matzah. They share it with their family.

During the meal, three matzot are used. A piece of the second one is hidden around the house by the parents. The child who finds it at the end of the meal gets a prize!

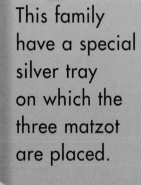

This family have a special silver tray on which the three matzot are placed.

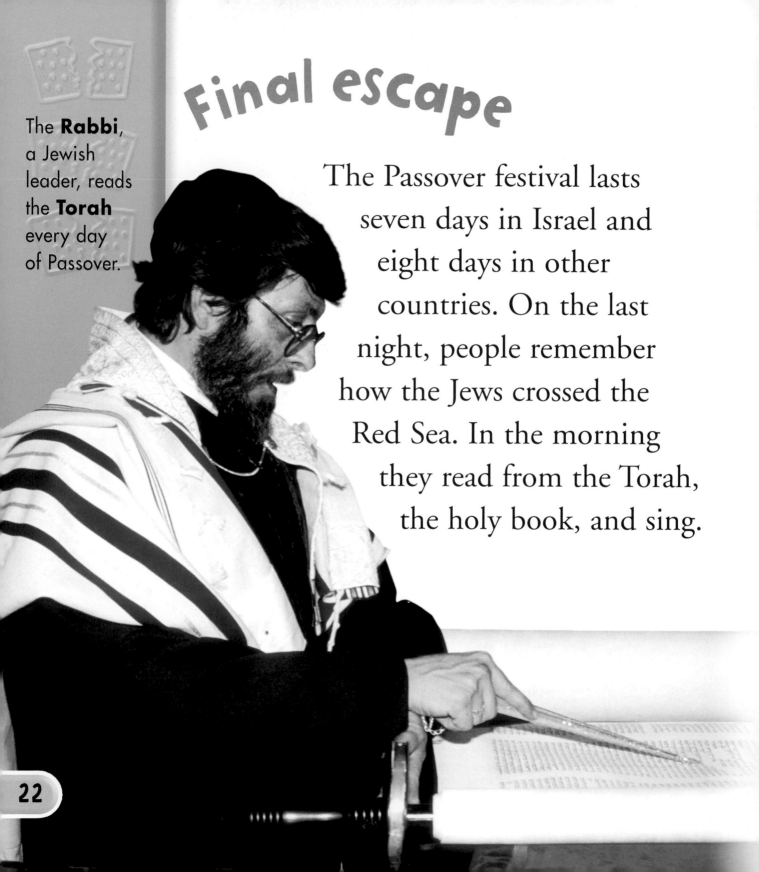

Final escape

The **Rabbi**, a Jewish leader, reads the **Torah** every day of Passover.

The Passover festival lasts seven days in Israel and eight days in other countries. On the last night, people remember how the Jews crossed the Red Sea. In the morning they read from the Torah, the holy book, and sing.

This picture shows Moses parting the Red Sea so that the Jews could escape from Egypt.

Then it's time to put away the special pots and pans. Another Passover festival is over.

Index and glossary

ancestors people that we are related to, from a long time ago
Haggadah the book used for telling the story of Passover
Hebrew the ancient Jewish language
kosher food that is prepared following Jewish law
matzah/matzot (plural) flat bread that is made without using yeast
Pharaoh an ancient Egyptian ruler
plague a pest or disease that spreads quickly over a wide area
pyramids ancient Egyptian tombs with sloping sides
Rabbi a Jewish leader
Seder the Jewish service and dinner at Passover
Torah the Jewish holy scrolls
yeast an ingredient used to make bread rise